Seeing Red

The Planet Mars

by Nancy Loewen   illustrated by Jeff Yesh

PICTURE WINDOW BOOKS

SAN DIEGO PUBLIC LIBRARY
LOGAN

Thanks to our advisers for their expertise, research, and advice:

Lynne Hillenbrand, Ph.D., Professor of Astronomy
California Institute of Technology

Terry Flaherty, Ph.D., Professor of English
Minnesota State University, Mankato

Editor: Jill Kalz
Designers: Amy Muehlenhardt and Melissa Kes
Page Production: Michelle Biedscheid
Art Director: Nathan Gassman
Associate Managing Editor: Christianne Jones
The illustrations in this book were created digitally.

Picture Window Books
5115 Excelsior Boulevard
Suite 232
Minneapolis, MN 55416
877-845-8392
www.picturewindowbooks.com

Copyright © 2008 by Picture Window Books
All rights reserved. No part of this book may
be reproduced without written permission from
the publisher. The publisher takes no responsibility
for the use of any of the materials or methods
described in this book, nor for the products thereof.

Printed in the United States of America.

All books published by Picture Window Books
are manufactured with paper containing at least
10 percent post-consumer waste.

Library of Congress Cataloging-in-Publication Data
Loewen, Nancy, 1964-
Seeing red : the planet Mars / by Nancy Loewen ; illustrated by Jeff Yesh.
p. cm. — (Amazing science. Planets)
Includes index.
ISBN 978-1-4048-3953-3 (library binding)
ISBN 978-1-4048-3962-5 (paperback)
1. Mars (Planet)—Juvenile literature. I. Yesh, Jeff, 1971- ill. II. Title.
QB641.L64 2008
523.43—dc22   2007032877

Table of Contents

The Red Planet

Mars is a small planet, but it can be seen from Earth with the naked eye. In ancient times, its reddish color made people think of blood. As a result, they named the planet after the Roman god of war.

Today we know that the color comes from iron, a metal found in the planet's soil.

4

FUN FACT

Of our solar system's eight planets—Mercury, Venus, Earth, Mars, Jupiter, Saturn, Uranus, and Neptune— Mars is the fourth planet from the sun. It is Earth's second-closest neighbor (Venus is closest).

Small and Cold

Mars is much smaller than Earth. Its diameter is about half of Earth's diameter. Only the planet Mercury is smaller.

Because Mars is farther from the sun than Earth is, the planet is much colder. The average temperature at the surface is around minus 80 degrees Fahrenheit (minus 62 degrees Celsius). The atmosphere, or layer of gases, around Mars is thin. It doesn't hold much heat.

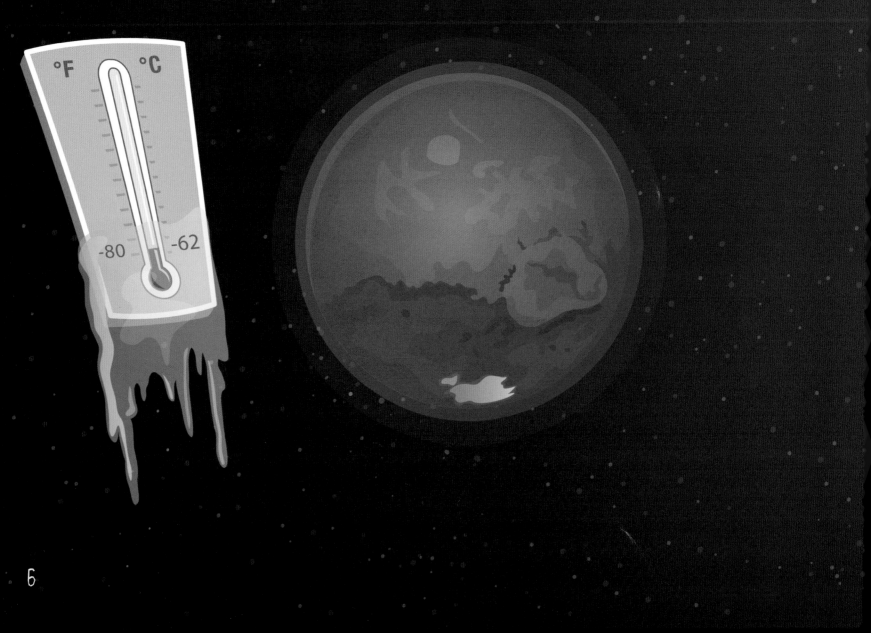

FUN FACT

The average temperature at Mars' surface is about the same as the average temperature at Earth's south pole.

Spinning and Circling

A day on Mars is only a little longer than a day on Earth. The planet takes 24 hours and 37 minutes to spin on its axis one time.

A Martian year, however, is almost twice as long as an Earth year. Mars takes 687 Earth days to orbit, or circle around, the sun. Earth takes just 365 days.

Jupiter

Uranus

Neptune

Saturn

Mercury

Venus

Earth

Mars

FUN FACT
Mars orbits the sun in an oval-shaped path.

EDITOR'S NOTE
In this illustration, the distances between planets
are not to scale. In reality, the distances between the
outer planets are much greater than the distances
between the inner planets.

Four Seasons

Mars is tilted on its axis, just a little more than Earth is. It is this tilt that causes Mars' four seasons. As Mars orbits the sun, some areas of the planet receive more light than other areas.

In the fall, temperatures start getting colder. Some of the carbon dioxide (a gas) in Mars' atmosphere freezes. It falls to the ground like snow. In the spring, temperatures start getting warmer. The carbon dioxide changes back into a gas and becomes part of the atmosphere again.

FUN FACT
Dust storms are common on Mars. Sometimes the storms cover the entire planet!

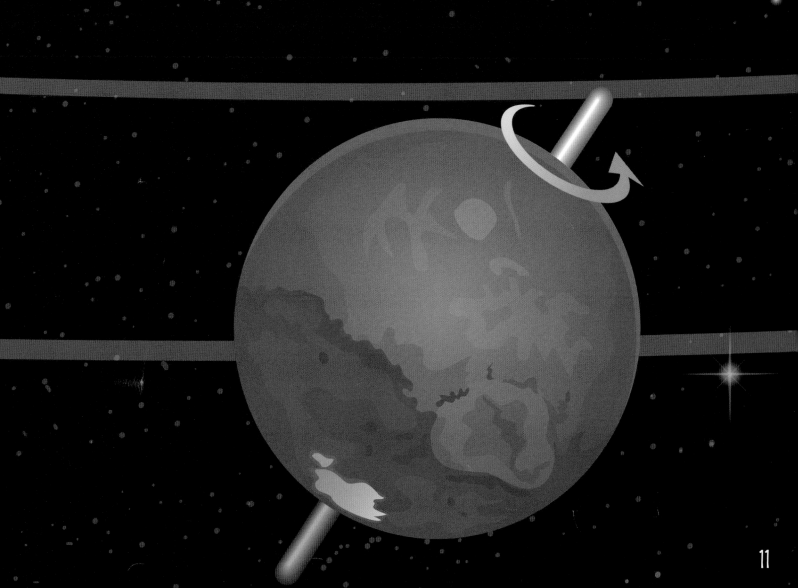

Like Earth, Mars has valleys and canyons. It has hills, mountains, and plains. It also has ice caps at its north and south poles. The northern cap is made of frozen water. The southern cap is made of frozen carbon dioxide.

FUN FACT

Many of the land features on Mars appear to have been carved out by water. But there is no liquid water on the planet at this time.

Dreaming of Mars

Is there life on Mars? And if so, what do Martians look like?
How do they act? Do they think and feel like us?
People have been asking these questions for
many, many years.

In the late 1800s, an American astronomer named Percival Lowell studied Mars through his telescope. He thought he saw canals filled with water. Canals are artificial, which means they have to be made by someone. So the astronomer started telling everyone that there were living beings on Mars!

When better telescopes were built, the truth came out: The canals weren't really there. Still, people continued to believe that there was life on Mars. Many authors wrote stories about what they believed Martians were like.

FUN FACT
Mars is one of the brightest objects in the night sky.

17

Martian Moons

Mars has two tiny moons called Deimos and Phobos. Scientists believe they were asteroids pulled into orbit by Mars' gravity.

Deimos takes about 30 Earth hours to complete its orbit around Mars. Phobos goes much faster. It takes about 8. Phobos is gradually getting closer to Mars, too. In about 50 million Earth years, it could crash onto Mars and break apart.

Deimos

Phobos

FUN FACT
Deimos (Terror) and Phobos (Panic) were named after a pair of horses in Greek mythology. The horses pulled the chariot of the Greek god Ares.

Still Searching

We know that no alien beings live on Mars. But many scientists believe that the conditions for life may once have existed there.

On Earth, we're discovering tiny creatures living in places of great heat or cold. Perhaps similar creatures live on Mars.

Is there life on Mars? No one knows for sure. But scientists are doing all they can to find out!

FUN FACT

More spacecraft have been sent to Mars than to any other planet. They have all been unmanned, however. No human being has ever landed on Mars.

- a place to spread out

What you do:

1. Have each person pick the role he or she wants to play: Mars, Phobos, Deimos, or the timekeeper.

2. Mars should stand in a central spot. Phobos should stand three steps away from Mars. Deimos should stand nine steps away from Mars. The timekeeper should stand off to the side.

3. Now it's time to practice your moves with the help of the timekeeper. Try each move individually at first, so you know how fast to go. Mars should stand in place and turn, making a complete circle in 24 seconds. Phobos should walk around Mars once every 8 seconds. Deimos should walk around Mars once every 30 seconds.

4. Try doing the moves all together. See if you can keep going for several minutes.

In this activity, Mars was rotating, but it wasn't orbiting. The real planet would be orbiting around the sun at the same time. And the moons would be rotating, too. Try spinning and walking at the same time. You'll probably end up in a major space crash, but at least you'll have fun!

Fun Facts

- Mars is a terrestrial planet, along with Mercury, Venus, and Earth. It is made mostly of rock.

- Mars has the tallest mountain in the solar system. It is called Olympus Mons. It is three times taller than Mount Everest.

- The Valles Marineris is a very large set of canyons on Mars. It is as long as the United States!

- Dozens of spacecraft have been sent to Mars by many different countries. Because so many of them have had problems, researchers joke about a "Martian Curse."

- Mars' gravity is about 38 percent of Earth's. If you weigh 100 pounds (45 kilograms) on Earth, you would weigh 38 pounds (17 kg) on Mars.

Glossary

asteroid—a rock that circles around the sun

astronomer—a scientist who studies stars, planets, and other objects in space

atmosphere—the gases that surround a planet

axis—the center on which something spins, or rotates

canal—a man-made waterway

diameter—the distance of a line running from one side of a circle, through the center, and across to the other side

gravity—the force that pulls things down toward the surface of a planet

orbit—the path an object takes to travel around a star or planet; also, to travel around a star or planet

solar system—the sun and the bodies that orbit around it; these bodies include planets, dwarf planets, asteroids, and comets

telescope—a device with mirrors or lenses; a telescope makes faraway objects appear closer

To Learn More

More Books to Read

Adamson, Thomas K. *Mars.* Mankato, Minn.: Capstone Press, 2008.

Howard, Fran. *Mars.* Edina, Minn.: ABDO Pub., 2008.

Landau, Elaine. *Mars.* New York: Children's Press, 2008.

Ward, D.J. *Exploring Mars.* Minneapolis: Lerner Publications, 2007.

On the Web

FactHound offers a safe, fun way to find Web sites related to topics in this book. All of the sites on FactHound have been researched by our staff.

1. Visit *www.facthound.com*
2. Type in this special code: 1404839534
3. Click on the FETCH IT button.

Your trusty FactHound will fetch the best sites for you!

Index

Look for all of the books in the Amazing Science: Planets series:

Brightest in the Sky: The Planet Venus
Dwarf Planets: Pluto, Charon, Ceres, and Eris
Farthest from the Sun: The Planet Neptune
The Largest Planet: Jupiter
Nearest to the Sun: The Planet Mercury
Our Home Planet: Earth
Ringed Giant: The Planet Saturn
Seeing Red: The Planet Mars
The Sideways Planet: Uranus